A HUSBAND'S LITTLE BLACK BOOK

A
HUSBAND'S LITTLE
BLACK BOOK

Common Sense, Wit
and Wisdom For A
Better Marriage

Robert J. Ackerman, Ph.D.

Health Communications, Inc.®
Deerfield Beach, Florida

Publisher: Health Communications, Inc.
            3201 S.W. 15th Street
            Deerfield Beach, Florida 33442-8190

Cover photo and design by
Andrea Perrine Brower

To My Parents,
Who Have Been Married
For More Than 50 Years.

Introduction

After I said, "I do," I said, "What do I do?" Marriage licenses don't come with instructions. It wouldn't matter anyway. Most men I know don't read directions. That's why we can't program the VCR. After all, we secretly know that "Real men don't need directions." We would rather drive around for hours looking for our destination than ask for directions.

This book represents the collective wisdom I have heard over the years from both husbands and wives about what makes a good husband. It is not intended to teach you how to redo your life. It is about the everday things that make living with her better. I hope you enjoy reading it and that it makes you think about her. It is the little things we do that make the biggest difference. Enjoy each other!

*Share the TV
remote control.*

*Shampoo her hair
for her birthday.*

Don't eat potato chips in bed.

Put the toilet seat down.

Don't ask her how long she's been on the phone.

Men always want to be

a woman's first love;

women have a more subtle

instinct: what they like

is to be a man's

last romance.

—*Unknown*

Don't take more out of your relationship than you put in.

Go for a walk and
hold her hand.

Send her flowers on

an ordinary day.

*Take turns driving
the new car.*

Chains do not hold a marriage together. It is threads, hundreds of tiny threads which sew people together through the years. That's what makes a marriage last—more than passion or even sex.

— Simone Signoret

*Fix household
appliances without
muttering about how
they broke.*

If she wrecks the car,
ask her if she is all right
before you ask about
the car.

You don't need to understand her completely to love her completely.

Delete

"I told you so" from

your vocabulary.

Write down her

telephone messages

correctly.

Go grocery shopping with her.

Do the

grocery shopping

yourself.

Help her wrap the

Christmas presents.

*Buy the holiday and
birthday cards you send
to your parents.*

Marriage is our last,

best chance to grow up.

—Joseph Barth

Ask her about her day.

Don't give her advice

unless she asks for it.

Listen when

she talks about

her friends.

Visit her relatives, too.

Look through her

high school yearbook.

See a movie of her choosing, even if you don't want to see it.

Then in the marriage union, the independence of the husband and the wife will be equal, their dependence mutal, and their obligations reciprocal.

—*Lucretia Mott*

Take her to bed

and just hold her.

When you're wrong

admit it.

One of the best things

about marriage is

that it gets young people

to bed at a decent hour.

—M. M. Musselman

Cook for her

when she's sick.

Laugh at her jokes.

Be honest, but don't tell her things that might hurt her feelings.

Share the last

bottle of soda.

Pick up your

dirty clothes.

Get out of bed first
on cold mornings and
turn up the heat.

*A woman is the only
thing that I am afraid of
that I know will not
hurt me.*

— *Abraham Lincoln*

Rinse the sink

after you shave.

If you win

the game you're playing,

don't gloat.

Past relationships
are better left in
the past.

Help decorate

the Christmas tree.

Let there be spaces in

your togetherness.

—Kahlil Gibran

Do the laundry —and

don't mix the whites

with the darks.

Start a fire in the fireplace

on cold winter nights.

Only the strongest of men

are gentle.

*Love does not consist
in gazing at each other,
but in looking together
in the same direction.*

—Antoine de Saint-Exupéry

Take her away overnight without the kids.

Take turns taking the children to the doctor's office when they are sick.

Don't put your wife on a pedestal; she doesn't want to be that far away.

When you're sick,

go to the doctor.

When you're lost, stop and ask for directions.

I can live for two months

on a good compliment.

—Mark Twain

Remember her
favorite color.

Give her praise.

Take turns.

Talk to her calmly.

Be polite.

Don't bring up her old boyfriends.

Rudeness is

the weak man's imitation

of strength.

—*Eric Hoffer*

*Call her in the middle
of the day just to say,
"Hello."*

Talk with her when you're

worried about money.

Help her put her clothes back on. Many people will help you take your clothes off, but only a few will help you put them back on.

*Go into the delivery room
with her and
be part of the birth of
your children.*

Make Mother's Day

a special day for her.

Find a moment alone with her on New Year's Eve.

A handful of patience is worth more than a bushel of brains.

—*Dutch proverb*

Learn to argue fairly.
Don't use phrases that
begin with "You always,"
or "You never."

If you feel empty when she's away, tell her when she gets back.

Be on time for dinner.

A bull does not enjoy fame

in two herds.

—*Rhodesian proverb*

Remember, she married you

so don't ask her to be logical!

Take turns balancing

the checkbook.

Discuss your childrens'
requests with your wife before
you give them an answer.

Remember that arguments have three sides—his, hers and the facts.

No one ever wins a fight.

Never cut what you can untie.

—Joseph Joubert

Do you want to be happy or do you want to be right?

*Don't say anything about
her weight gain and
she won't say anything
about your hair loss.*

The test of a man or woman's breeding is how they behave in a quarrel.

—George Bernard Shaw

If you abuse your wife,

you have no relationship.

Marriage requires you to create many definitions of love.

Pick up the kids after school.

Give her neck rubs when she comes home from work.

If she can't start the lawn mower, blame it on the mower.

Fill up the empty ice cube tray.

When I was young, I kissed my first woman and smoked my first cigarette on the same day. Believe me, never since have I wasted any more time on tobacco.

— Arturo Toscanini

Husbands should take
time for themselves,
but not too much.

A husband's silence often says more than we think. It is better to explain ourselves.

Open the door for her.

*Clean your own fish when
you go fishing.*

Always ask her to dance.

Show her respect.

Any married man should forget his mistakes — no use two people remembering the same thing.

—Duane Dewel

Keep her secrets.

Go car shopping together.

Worship together.

Be faithful, and remember,
it doesn't matter where you
get your appetite as long as
you eat at home.

If you don't want to do something, tell her why.

Bake chocolate chip cookies together on a Sunday afternoon.

Loneliness and the feeling of

being unwanted is

the most terrible poverty.

—*Mother Teresa*

Watch a sunset together

in silence.

Take her to the park and push her on the swing.

Practice patience on a regular basis.

She's your partner, so stand up for her.

Don't criticize her family.

Polish her toenails.

Learn to cook three

different dinners.

*Men always talk about
the most important things to
perfect strangers.*

—G. K. Chesterton

If you want to know

what's inside of her,

listen to what she says

and she will unfold.

*Take turns cleaning
the bathroom.*

He has a right to criticize,

who has a heart to help.

— *Abraham Lincoln*

Surprise her with

tickets to the theatre.

If you go away, give her the telephone number where you can be reached.

You can't drink your way

to a good marriage.

The most important thing a father can do for his children is to love their mother.

—Theodore Hesburgh

Look at your wedding pictures on your anniversary.

If you forget her birthday, have a good excuse. If you forget your anniversary— move out of town!

Replace the toilet paper

when it runs out.

Just think of all her unmentionables hanging in the bathroom as tools hanging in the garage.

Never go into her purse

unless she tells you to.

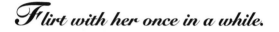

Flirt with her once in a while.

Where you used to be, there is a hole in the world, which I find myself constantly walking around in the daytime, and falling into at night. I miss you like hell.

—Edna St. Vincent Millay

Learn to be tolerant.

It will reduce your

blood pressure.

It is more important to go together than it is to know where you are going.

Don't hate, it's too big a burden to bear.

—Martin Luther King, Jr.

Order something for her from the Victoria's Secret catalog.

She has many needs,

but the most important

is to be needed.

Never swear at her.

*Don't spend a lot of money
without talking it over
with her first.*

*If you find yourself
getting angry with her,
just walk away
for a while.*

Turn off the football game
during Thanksgiving dinner.

If the phone rings when you are making love, don't answer it. Who could be more important?

Pay attention when she asks,

"Are you listening to me?"

When there is nothing left to be said sometimes a hug goes a long way.

Make sure you keep

your promises.

*Take a lot of family
pictures and arrange them
in a photo album.*

Keep a picture of her

in your wallet.

Surprise her by cleaning the house while she is gone.

Keep your standards

to yourself.

Let her drive and you

deal with the kids.

Don't rush her when she's telling you a story.

Love her for who she is,

not for what you would

like her to be.

See everything; overlook a great deal; correct a little.

—Pope John XXIII

Make her laugh a lot.

The greatest danger to
marriage is apathy.

While she is in the shower,

warm her bath towel

in the dryer.

Fill the bathtub with hot water and bubble bath for her, light a candle, fill a glass of white wine —then leave her alone.

Some things might not be

a big deal to you,

but they are to her.

Respect her feelings.

Spend more time with

your children.

Marriage 101

Today's lesson is priorities:

Wife, children, job.

Wife, children, job.

Wife, children, job.

Any questions?

Learn to receive.

Don't resent her girlfriends.

If listening to another person

is an art, become an artist.

Write her a love letter, but be careful about what you promise. You don't want to be guilty of male fraud.

Take her shopping for a new outfit.

Sometimes you will get

the last words,

but they might be

"Yes, dear."

Also by
Robert J. Ackerman, Ph.D.

Silent Sons

Perfect Daughters

Children Of Alcoholics

Too Old To Cry

Abused No More

Let Go And Grow

Recovery Resource Guide

Growing In The Shadow

About the author

Robert J. Ackerman, Ph.D., is the husband of Kimberly Roth Ackerman, the father of three children and professor of sociology at Indiana University of Pennsylvania. And he tries to keep his life in that order.